TODDLER THEOLOGY
Childlike Faith for Everyone

written by

Cathy D. Dudley

illustrated by Matt Ramsey

Second Edition, 2018

ISBN: 978-0-692-12639-4

Library of Congress Control Number: 2018906091

Blessing2UPublishing
P.O. Box 854, Fincastle, VA 24090

Printed in the United States of America

cathyddudley.com

This Book was especially written
for my precious Grandchildren
Janey
Austin
Naomi
Cora Lou
Sawyer
Leo
"twinkle in someone's eye"

This book is dedicated to
All Parents and Grandparents

Hi! My name is Jesus. I live in heaven with my Father. His name is God. The Holy Spirit lives with us too. Heaven is way, way up above the clouds. It's a really beautiful and happy place.

Let me tell you about God. He can do wonderful things that no one else can. We call them miracles. Long ago, He made the world and everything in it. And guess what? He still does miracles today – like painting pretty sunsets ... and growing flowers from little seeds ... and even knitting you together before you were born. That means He's YOUR Father in heaven too!

I know you can't see me, but I'd like to be your friend. I'm standing at the door to your heart.

It'll be fun to get to know me. I have lots of gifts for you! They aren't presents you can open. They are promises that will keep you smiling, even on gloomy days. My very favorite is the home I'm making for you in heaven.

Did you know I used to live on this earth? One of God's greatest miracles was sending me down from heaven on the very first Christmas long ago. I was born a tiny baby ... just like you. How about that? Christmas is My Birthday!

When I grew up, I used my awesome powers to heal sick people. I was a teacher, too, and taught everybody to love God — and be kind and good to one another. People followed me wherever I went. Even the little children, like you, would come listen to me tell my stories. We would laugh, and they'd take turns sitting on my lap.

Then, when I was 33 years old, God gave me a really special job. I went to the cross. It was there that I paid the price for you and the whole world to be able to travel to heaven. It hurt a lot and took all my blood to buy tickets for everyone, but I wanted to do it. Why? Because I love you. And I knew nobody could ever be good enough to get a ticket on their own. That's why people call me the Savior of the world!

And listen to this miracle. I didn't stay dead! After 3 days, God raised me back to life. Pretty amazing, huh?

I'll be keeping your ticket to heaven very, very safe until you're ready to ask me for it. Then I'll know you believe in Me and My Story. That's called having faith.

Faith starts out tiny and gets bigger whenever we spend time together ... like praying. Prayer is a good way to talk to me. And I never sleep – so I'm always listening for you – in the morning, at mealtime, when you're playing, and especially at bedtime. Maybe you can tell me "Good Night" when you get tucked in.

You can learn more about me in the Bible. My same stories are written there for you to read today. The Holy Spirit will help you understand the words so we can feel closer. As a matter of fact, another name for the Holy Spirit is The Helper. He's invisible, like me, and very strong ... so He can help you turn away from things that are bad. I'm sure you'll like Him.

So, NOW do you know how much I Love You? I hope you decide to make me your friend ... your best friend. I can't wait to do things with you!

And, remember, I'm always right there beside you. Just whisper my name. You'll see!